On A Rainbow

Words & Music by Tom Fletcher

On a Rainbow

Official London 2012 Mascot Song

Words and music by Tom Fletcher.
Arranged for piano, voice and guitar.

Manufactured under license by
Universal Music Publishing Group.
20 Fulham Broadway
London
SW6 1AH.

Made in the U.K.

£ _____ Code: 15

AM1005224

ISBN 978-1-78038-691-1

9 781780 386911